As a historical painter. . . I had to record the crises, the calamities, the hunger, thirst, sweat, toil of the people settling into an untamed country. This I feel is nothing to be ashamed of. On the contrary, it glorifies the courage, the service, the toughness. . . William Kurelek

They Sought a New World

Paintings © 1985, The Estate of the late William Kurelek

Text © 1985, Tundra Books

Published in Canada by Tundra Books, Montreal H3G 1R4
ISBN 0-88776-172-0 hardcover 10, 9, 8, 7, 6, 5, 4, 3
ISBN 0-88776-213-1 paperback 10, 9, 8, 7, 6, 5, 4, 3, 2

Published in the United States by Tundra Books of Northern New York,
Plattsburgh, N.Y. 12901

Canadian Cataloguing in Publication Data

Kurelek, William, 1927-1977

They sought a new world

ISBN 0-88776-172-0

1. Canada — Emigration and immigration — History — Juvenile literature.
2. United States — Emigration and immigration — History — Juvenile literature.
3. Canada — Population — Ethnic groups — History — Juvenile literature.
4. United States — Population — Ethnic groups — History — Juvenile literature.
5. Europeans — Canada — History — Juvenile literature. 6. Europeans — United
States — History — Juvenile literature. I. Engelhart, Margaret II. Title.

JV7220.K97 1985   j971'.004   C85-090060-3

Paintings in the Estate of the late William Kurelek are controlled by the Isaacs Gallery, Toronto, Ontario, Canada.

Paintings reproduced in full or in detail in this book come from the following collections: *The Polish Canadians* © 1981, Estate of the late William Kurelek, published by Tundra Books - pages 4, 10 (detail), 12, 13, 14, 15 (detail), 20-21 (detail), 27, 28-29, 30 (detail), 32 (detail), 38, 40-41, 42 (detail), 44, 46-47 (detail); The Irish Series - page 7; *Jewish Life in Canada*, © 1976, William Kurelek & Abraham J. Arnold, published by Hurtig Publishers - pages 8, 16, 17, 35; *Fields* © 1976, William Kurelek, published by Tundra Books - all details pages 18, 22, 24, 25, 26; from private collections - pages 34 (detail), 36.

The quotations from William Kurelek are taken from the following sources: Pages 6, 26, 31, 33, 37 *Someone With Me, the Autobiography of William Kurelek*, © 1980, published by McClelland & Stewart, Limited; Page 24 original edition of *Someone With Me*, © 1973, Center for Improvement of Undergraduate Education, Cornell University; Pages 1, 9, 19, 25 *Kurelek's Vision of Canada* © 1983, Robert McLaughlin Gallery, Oshawa and the Estate of William Kurelek published by Hurtig; Page 25 *Kurelek's Canada*, © 1975 Pagurian Press; Pages 12, 20 *The Polish Canadians*, © 1981 Estate of the late William Kurelek published by Tundra Books; Pages 11, 31, 43 *Lumberjack*, © 1974 William Kurelek published by Tundra Books. The account quoted by William Kurelek of *One Man's Experience* on page 20 is taken from the book *History and Integration of Poles in Canada*, 1967 by William Boeslaus Makowski.

Foreign Editions:
1985 Dutch: Uitgeverij C. de Vries-Brouwers p.v.b.a., Antwerp, Belgium

1986 Danish: Host & Sons Forlag, Copenhagen, Denmark
    Norwegian: Det Norske Samlaget, Oslo, Norway
    Finnish: Weilin + Göös, Espoo, Finland
    Swedish: Carlsen if, Stockholm, Sweden

Printed in Belgium.

They Sought A New World

The story of European immigration to North America

Paintings and comments by **William Kurelek**

additional text by Margaret S. Engelhart

A Tundra Book

Arriving in the New World: Full of hope, a pioneering couple build their first shelter in the wilderness.

Everyone living in North America is an immigrant or the descendant of an immigrant.

The first peoples to come to North America probably walked here, across a land bridge that once existed between Asia and Alaska. They were either following animals or searching for them, and they brought their way of living and their skills with them. They had weapons for hunting and fishing; they knew how to make clothing from animal skins and how to build shelters from whatever was handy: skins, trees, earth, ice or snow. Our native Indians and Inuit are believed to be descendants of these first settlers.

No one knows who first came to North America by sailing across the Atlantic Ocean, possibly sailors who had lost their way. We do know of early visitors from Scandinavia and explorers from many parts of Europe. They were followed by settlers and soldiers from England and France as the two countries fought each other through the 1700s for control of the North American continent.

By 1815, when the wars between England and France finally stopped, the United States had broken away from England and become an independent nation and the British had taken Canada from the French. Both countries had huge empty lands in the West and needed farmers; both countries needed workers for their factories, mines and forests. They wanted immigrants to come.

And from all over Europe people came, some 50 million of them during the next 150 years, 37 million to the United States, nearly 13 million to Canada. They were not the only immigrants to contribute to the multiracial, multinational, multireligious and multiethnic society that is the particular strength of North American democracies. Immigrants who came from Asiatic countries, from Hispanic America, and from Africa (most particularly those who were brought, tragically and involuntarily, from that continent) — all have fashioned a "new" world by insisting ideals of freedom and equality be practiced. Theirs are different histories, just as the histories of the native Indians and Inuits differ.

Here we show a little of what it meant to be a European immigrant, using the paintings and writings of a great artist who was himself the son of such an immigrant.

Margaret S. Engelhart

Why they left Europe

Why did they leave home to make the long frightening trip across the ocean to live among strangers in an alien land? The reasons were many.

They left because wars and revolution had destroyed their homes. Because the land they lived on could no longer feed them. Because crops failed and they were hungry. Because families were large and there was not enough land to divide among all the children. Because they might spend their lives working on someone else's land and never own any of their own. Because they were forced to serve in armies against their will. Because they could not worship God as they wished. Because they belonged to a minority that was denied rights given to others. Because they could not speak out against those in power without being jailed or killed.

Some young men came simply because they were restless and wanted adventure, and the American continent seemed big and different and exciting. And some young women came to marry a fiancé or to find a husband.

Most came because they felt they had no choice. As one immigrant woman explained, "We came because we were poor."

North America offered hope.

. . . Although Grandfather intended to divide his land among his three sons, Father being second eldest, wasn't satisfied with his smaller portion. At war's end, an agent from the British Cunard Steamship Line appeared in the village and soon persuaded my father to migrate. . . Besides the lure of owning land, Father wanted to escape conscription into the Rumanian army. Draftees returning to the village had told of beatings and other humiliations at the hands of the officers.W.K.

Shipping and railway companies from both the United States and Canada openly advertised to take people to North America. They made money from every person they transported, and their agents worked hard through northern and eastern Europe. They put up posters. They visited farm areas and urged whole villages to come. They promised religious groups land and freedom to set up their own communities. They opened offices in cities to give out information. They described North America as a paradise.

But the information given was only half the truth. They promised it would be easy to find work. They did not tell how hard that work would be. They promised free land. They did not tell how difficult farming that land would be.

Sometimes emigration was encouraged by the home country who wanted to get rid of its poor. Orphans and children abandoned by their parents were transported in large numbers to become servants and cheap farm labor. From 1869 to 1930 between 80,000 and 100,000 British children were brought to Canada in this way.

But some countries did not want their citizens to leave. They needed them for the army. When Germany passed laws against advertising for immigrants, steamship agents worked secretly. They were paid by the Canadian government for every person they convinced: five dollars for a farmer and domestic servant and two dollars for each of their children. In spite of this Germans came in large numbers, and next to the British and Irish became the largest immigrant group in the 19th century.

Reaching a port where one could board a ship was the first problem. Sometimes whole villages traveled together, sometimes a few families. Sometimes a religious group with its leader. Men might make the trip alone. Single women usually traveled with relatives. Those from central Europe moved on foot, or by wagon or train, to the seaports of northern Europe, to Hamburg or Bremen. Many traveled at night, fearing they would be caught and arrested, and the men and older boys forced into the army. Scandinavians frequently sailed first to Hull or Newcastle in England, then moved on to Liverpool to find a ship bound for North America.

The Long Voyage. Weeks crowded into the holds of ships was the terrifying introduction to the New World.

Arriving on the Prairies: When they saw the vast emptiness, did they wonder if they should have come?

. . . its enormity dwarfs and dominates life, all life, both man and animal, whether it crawls, walks, or flies over its surface, or tries to leave its mark on it, such as dwelling places or modes of travel. There is an obvious contrast in this respect between our country and Europe, for example, where man over thousands of years has come to dominate nature, in fact, to nearly completely subdue her. . . W.K.

Getting to the new land

Most of the immigrants came from farms. Few had ever been far from their native village. Even fewer had been to sea. They did not know what to expect and were not prepared for the trip.

If they journeyed before 1850, the ship was a sailing craft and the trip might take as long as six to eight weeks. Even when the sea voyage could be made in two or three weeks, it was sheer misery.

Many of the early ships were not built to carry passengers. The owners, anxious to make as much money as possible from each voyage, treated the travelers like cargo. They were crowded into the hold of the ship where they slept on bunks that might be three layers high. Food was poor: wheat flour, tea, rice, oatmeal, molasses and hard biscuit. Sometimes there was not enough fresh water. If they washed themselves, there might not be enough water to drink. They were often sick from the tossing of the ship, from fear of its sinking, from the crying of children, from the smells and the noise, and from watching the suffering of those around them. There was no place to be alone. Years later many would recall to their children and grandchildren how relieved they had been to set foot on land.

But now new problems faced them. Many knew neither English nor French, the languages of the early settlers. Those who already had relatives or friends living in the new country were fortunate. There was someone to help them find work and a place to live, to explain the new customs and laws and to ease the loneliness. Often immigrants stayed in the city where they landed just to be among people from their own country. Men who arrived alone were encouraged to go West or North to tough jobs where women were not wanted: to work on railroads, in mines and in lumber camps.

Those families promised farmland had still more travel ahead of them. In the United States, the trip westward for the first settlers was by horse and covered wagon; their hardship has been dramatized in many books and films. In Canada, railways opened the West to settlers, and that meant days and nights sitting upright in uncomfortable railway cars that took them farther and farther into an empty land.

Some would be so disappointed and so overwhelmed by problems, or feel so lonely for their families and friends, that they gave up and returned to their European homelands.

But most stayed and struggled through.

Workers Wanted. Smokestacks rising all over North America meant new industries welcoming immigrants.

Finding work

As the cities of North America grew, so too did the number of factories. For them the immigrant — Irish or Polish, later eastern European and Italian — was an ideal worker. He might not be skilled but he was eager to learn and willing to work hard for long hours at very little pay in dark, dirty buildings. But the harder the immigrant worked and pleased his employer, the more he might be resented by other workers who feared they would lose their jobs to the new "cheap labor." Gradually as the years passed and immigrants felt more secure in their new country, they joined other workers and turned to the trade union movement to get them fair wages and better working conditions.

Steel mills and mines opened up everywhere and attracted many immigrant families. Often the towns were built by the companies who owned and controlled everything from the houses people lived in to the places where they were forced to shop. The employer decided the rents and store prices workers had to pay, as well as their wages.

Women immigrants were offered low-paying work of another kind. Although most had never worked outside their homes in Europe, they accepted jobs in textile mills and clothing factories. They also worked as servants in other people's houses where they cleaned, cooked and cared for the children. If the servant was unmarried, she was expected to "live in." If she had a family of her own, she did "day work," and returned at night to look after her own house and family.

Male immigrants were expected to do the most physically demanding jobs for the lowest pay. They were also expected to go wherever there was work available, no matter how isolated the area or how long they must be away from family and friends. Building and repairing the railroads that spanned the continent was one such job. Lumbering was another. Forests were once everywhere. It is said that a squirrel could travel from Texas to Canada by jumping from tree to tree, without ever having to touch the ground. Wood was the main material for building, and later for the newspaper industry. As the vast stands of timber in the United States were cut into heavily before 1900, Canada became the main supply source for the continent. Until well after World War II work in lumber camps remained the first job for many immigrants to Canada.

. . . we had to face the hard bush reality of lumber jack life . . . of clouds of mosquitoes and black flies; of tripping from fatigue over twigs and fallen trees; of cords falling apart, and of blades and handles snapping; of limbs nicked by saw and ax cuts; of heavy perspiration followed by thirsts so fierce that even the little pools of soapy water in the muskeg looked tempting. . .W.K.

One immigrant would find work in a new industry or construction site and then recruit others of his countrymen to join him. In this way, concentration of certain nationalities developed in certain industries and certain cities, such as the breweries, stockyards, shipyards, cement factories and grain elevators.

. . . I once worked in those giant elevators myself, as a construction worker, rather than a handler of grain, although I'd shoveled plenty of it on my father's farm. . . it was the time of the Great Depression. . . Those who did have employment and families to support were always fearful of losing their jobs. In some cases, they submitted to bad working conditions from which they might have rebelled otherwise. . . W.K.

In Dark Holds: Immigrants shoveling grain in dark elevators wear masks to avoid breathing dust.

Sharing News from Home: Rooming houses provided cheap housing and companionship for newcomers.

Men who came alone and took work in the cities lived in rooming houses with other immigrants from their country. When they saved enough money to send for their wife and family or to get married, they moved to flats or tenement houses usually among others who spoke the same language. All large American and Canadian cities have sections known by the nationality of those who gathered there: "Little Italy," Germantown, the Polish quarter, Swede town, the Irish section, the Jewish quarter. Towns founded by immigrants often took place-names from their homeland. London, Paris, Rome, Berlin, Aberdeen, Geneva, Dublin, Vienna, Amsterdam, Florence, Warsaw, Moscow — these and the names of thousands of smaller European centers dot the map of North America.

In Lumber Camps. Immigrants cut trees by hand, using a cant hook to move giant trunks.

14

On the Railroads: Laying tracks and repairing them — especially in remote areas — was immigrant work.

Fishermen could find work on the east coast, and experienced sailors in merchant shipping. Artisans, cabinetmakers, carpenters, mechanics and others trained through lengthy European apprenticeships were in demand everywhere, although many would complain that speed was more appreciated in North America than quality work.

Tailors who knew how to make men's suits and coats found work easily, but the pay was pitifully small. Women's and children's clothing, once sewn by mothers at home, came to be made more and more in factories. These "sweatshops" might be no more than one or two crowded rooms in a slum. Here men or women cut and sewed, elbow to elbow, for twelve or more hours a day, six days a week. Since they were paid only for work done, they received no money at all if they were sick. In spite of the long hours and the unhealthy work places, many women were proud of their pay check, small as it was, and the feeling of independence it gave them. The successive waves of immigrants from different nations are reflected in the history of the textile and clothing industries, as earlier immigrants learned the new language, moved on to better jobs and left their places to the newcomers.

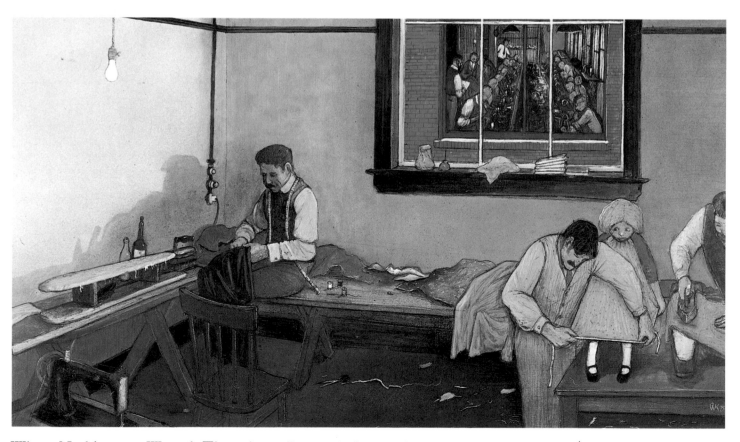

Where Nothing was Wasted: The suit a tailor made for the father would end up clothing the children.

A World in Miniature: The village store tried to be — and sell — everything to everyone.

In small towns, the general store sold a little of everything and gave comfort to everyone. Even more than the church, it acted as a community center for it was open to all. The storekeeper was often postmaster and seen as a government information officer. Whether he was an immigrant himself or native born, he was expected to know the latest news and to explain the latest laws. He might be asked to translate and to write letters, to advise on tools or shoes, to suggest medicines for the sick and to be patient and impartial with all inquiries. His store was also an informal employment office, where laborers were told what farmers might need help. As the size of farms grew, many immigrants became itinerant or seasonal workers, moving from one part of the country to the other, according to the different harvest times.

As Far as the Eye Could See: Blue skies and green fields promised the fulfillment of every dream.

The dream of owning land

One of the freedoms promised immigrants was the chance to own land. In many European countries, aristocratic families controlled huge estates and no matter how hard a peasant worked, it would always be for someone else. Farmers who did own land often found it too small to feed their families or to divide up among their sons. Marching armies, crop failure, plagues and famine increased feelings of hopelessness.

To such farmers, the empty land of Canada and the United States seemed a dream come true. They could get it for nothing or next to nothing. All they need do was clear it, build a house on it, farm it or raise cattle or sheep and they and their children would be secure. They did not suspect the hardships, the loneliness, the disappointments as crops were lost through drought and disease.

In the United States, settlers faced another threat: attacks by Indians trying to protect their territories and hunting lands from the relentless spread westward. In Canada, relationships with the native Indians were better — missionaries had worked with them, voyageurs and trappers had married Indian women, and treaties had arranged rights of peaceful settlement. But immigrant farmers on the Canadian prairies had their own peculiar problems such as the shortness of the growing season and the extreme winter cold.

The United States and Canada welcomed immigrants from each other's country as well as from Europe. During the 19th century, the movement was heavily southward and in some years Canada lost more inhabitants to the United States than it gained through immigration. But by 1900, most of the free land in the United States was taken, while in Canada, where western settlement came only after the railways were built, there was still much available.

The Canadian government decided on a massive campaign to recruit farmers in the United States as well as in England and Europe. It opened immigration offices in several western American cities, sent 300 agents across the United States on recruiting trips, and brought American editors to the prairies to "sell" Canada. Within the six years from 1897-1903, the number moving northward went from 2,500 to 50,000 a year. Many in the United States sold farms they had developed, moved to Canada to get free land and used the income from their sale to build a better house or buy newer farm machinery. Not all of them stayed. Indeed some farmers went back and forth several times, as if there were no border.

One man's experience

"... I arrived in Edmonton in 1911 and found work in the city sewer system digging ditches. I was paid 10 cents an hour and worked there for two years. After I'd saved $60 I bought a homestead near Rochester, 85 miles north of Edmonton. At the end of each month I walked there and back. My first house was a shack made of tree branches. The second house was still only one room but had a large fireplace in the middle of it...

"I still had to work outside to buy necessary tools and utensils for the farm and house. Putting in 10 hours a day, 25 cents per hour, I was able to save up enough at last to bring over from Poland in 1914 my wife, daughter and two small sons. We all lived in that one room while I continued to walk 85 miles into the city...

"There were no schools either and the children learned only what their mother could teach them. All farm work was done by hand until 1917 when I saved enough to buy our first horse and a year later a second one. That same year we got our first cow too and when the railway came to Rochester we carried our farm produce there on our backs some eight miles distance. My daughter found employment as a domestic for six dollars a week and we saved four of these six dollars each week so I could repay the government the 60 dollars I'd borrowed from them..."
quoted by W.K.

20

Nature gives not a drop of comfort, can do nothing, will do nothing.

The single outstanding feature of prairie landscape ... just as of the ocean, is expanse ... and in that expanse are liberally laid out the basic elements of soil, sky, cloud, wind, grass, poplar bush, snow and sun... W.K.

The Long Walk: The account given here of the long walk to town to get provisions occurs frequently in the memoirs of immigrants to Canada, many of whom are still alive. Because they were so poor when they arrived, even the purchase of a horse and wagon had to be postponed. The first house was often a sod hut, warm in winter but very damp, where "when it rained three days outside, it rained five inside." The single-room hut that was usually put up next became the barn or chicken shed when the permanent house was finally built.

Much Yet to be Done: Cutting the trees down was only the first step in getting soil ready for seeding.

Clearing the land

Preparing the land for farming was the first and most difficult job. In the eastern part of the continent, the trees the farmer cut down usually became logs for his first house. But before he could plant, there was still much to be done. Tree stumps, rocks, stones and tangled roots had to be removed, all by hand. Families spent whole summers doing this, with every child expected to help as much as he was able. Today in many parts of the United States and Canada, you will see beautiful fences built from the rocks dug out of the land. They remain as the only monuments to the toil of the first settlers, since some of that land is no longer farmed. Sometimes after a farmer had cleared the land, planted it and struggled through several difficult years, he realized the soil was too poor, the land too hilly, the growing season too short for him ever to succeed. So he simply abandoned it and moved on.

Those who came in religious groups avoided one of the greatest hardships: loneliness. They could help each other clear, plant and build, could give comfort in times of illness or grief.

But most immigrant farmers came alone, or with their family. And for them the problems could be overwhelming and the loneliness heartbreaking. To anyone looking back, the astonishing thing is not that some gave up the struggle and returned to their home countries, but that so many stayed.

Even those who bought working farms had no guarantee of success. The gains of a few good years could be wiped out overnight. Storms and fires of great ferocity could burn a house, a barn or a field. If there was too much rain, the grain might rot. If there was not enough, it would dry up. Since there were few doctors and they might be far away, any sickness or accident could mean death. There were quarrels over land ownership, misunderstandings over money lending, and always fear of not being able to keep up mortgages or loan payments. These difficulties were often magnified for the immigrant who had to do everything in an unfamiliar language.

Farming never was easy. But the hardest time of all for immigrant farmers, and for all western farmers in both countries, came during the Great Depression of the 1930s. As if the general poverty and unemployment were not enough, there were several years of drought throughout the West. Farmers saw their land seized by banks and mortgage companies, their families evicted from the homes they had gone through so much to build. Photographs of such families moving away in wagons or old cars, with children looking sadly out from around mattresses, chairs, pots and pans, are among the saddest of the decade.

Children's Work: Boys or girls were given the job of bringing cows home and doing the actual milking.

Because so many immigrants had come from lives of great hardship in Europe and been forced to work from a very early age, they often made the same demands on their children.

. . . John and I, small and scrawny as we were, had to step into a man's shoes. I was twelve, John only ten years old, but Father impatiently dismissed the age factor: "When I was nine in the Old Country, I had to plow all day by myself and I couldn't even see the furrow properly because the plow was taller than me. . ."

And a year later —

. . . As an eleven year old, John could hardly adjust the binder wing lever. To offset all the time lost on breakdowns, we cut well into the night till the moon rose. . .we tumbled into bed so tired we didn't even bother washing or changing. Yet the next morning we were expected to get up at 6 a.m. . . .to fetch the cows for milking. . .I still remember my pained wrists after milking ten or twenty cows. . . W.K.

Children's Play: A mound of newmown hay was an excuse for games, a welcome pause from work.

. . . people were poor, but there were ways of making our own fun even in those hard times. . . W.K.

. . . I used to feel the call of the great, free, flat bogland to the east of our farm. I found myself walking or cycling out on it whenever freed from farm work. Even though my father didn't actually own a single foot of it, it still said to me, "You and I belong to each other. . ." W.K.

Farm children had to make their own fun. There was little money for toys or sports equipment. Fishing rods, baseball bats and hockey sticks were often homemade. A pond, stream or river became a swimming pool. An old horse, gentle and obliging, could be ridden by one or two children at a time, without a saddle. A field of fresh snow became a playground. There were rabbits and gophers to catch. And after a summer of farm work, returning to school seemed like going on vacation.

. . . it was a summer morning when Father noticed a peculiar yellow cloud approaching from the east over the bogland. The crops stood green, not too tall, but promising nevertheless. By evening the cloud had arrived. It was grasshoppers, billions of them, a flying, munching, crawling blanket that settled on the crops, the grass, even the leaves of the trees. . . Father in that darkest hour seemed stronger, more serenely fatalistic, than I'd expected him to be. I recall his drawing the family together after supper that fall and consoling us: "Never mind, we'll try one more year here and if that also fails then I know of another farm east of here that we can make a fresh start on."

As if the grasshoppers hadn't been enough, we suffered a minor drought that year as well. . . W.K.

At the Mercy of Nature: A single spark could destroy a field and wipe away hope for a harvest.

In Sickness and in Health: When the mother fell ill, this father plowed with his baby strapped to his back.

The immigrant farmer started with so little, he could not afford to hire anyone to help him.
He did everything alone, his wife helping when she could. Illness could be disastrous.

This farmer *"fell seriously ill while digging a well. After he recovered his wife was hospitalized. . .*
Their third son. . .was then a one-year-old baby. With no one else available to care for the child,
Josef had to carry him whenever he went into the fields, plowing, disking or cultivating.
"One day a horse at the disks bolted and the jerk threw the baby in front of the machine. He'd
have been chopped up had the other horse not been placid and stayed put. . . The trauma of his
near death was such that the farmer simply unhitched the horses, left the field, and never touched
it again. The next year he auctioned off the farm. . ." W.K.

A Funeral Far from the Homeland: The saddest time of all for immigrants — the time when they felt most alone — was when a loved one died, and the relatives that could comfort them were far away. Many friendships with neighbors began at such times.

28

. . . *The coffins of the first pioneers were no more than birchbark woven over two poles. On this primitive stretcher the body was placed, wrapped in a white sheet. . . The farm burial plot (church cemeteries came later) resembled the Old Country one. . . W.K.*

The Game of Fox and Geese: After a snowfall, the yard outside the one-room school became a playground.

30

Learning to be a child of the New World

After a summer of work, school came as a welcome change to farm children. But if one was the child of an immigrant, it meant new problems.

. . . A few days later began the most traumatic experience of my pre-adult life. . . starting school . . . The reason was language embarrassment. We would immediately start chattering in Ukrainian only to discover there was a kind of unwritten taboo on any language but English in a public school . . . The teacher was staring at me. Then it hit me! I'd used the wrong language. I clammed up immediately and wished with all my heart that it was possible to sink beneath the floor. . . Within a few days we found we'd been singled out for bullying by the older boys. . . Name-calling and fists were the two main weapons. . . W.K.

It was not only in school that immigrant children had problems. They had them at home too. As they grew older they were caught between two worlds: between the customs and values of the Old World followed at home and those of the New World learned from schoolmates and friends.

As they learned to speak English without an accent, they grew to be more American or Canadian than European. Some became ashamed of the way their parents talked and dressed and resented the rules their parents set. Arguments over small things were frequent — the hour a child should go to bed or be home at night, the length of a dress or style of haircut. Quarrels often grew more bitter as the children reached adolescence — over their choice of friends, over the religion or nationality of those they dated, over the course of education they should follow. The bickering wore out both young and old.

Parents who felt they had gone through so much and worked so hard to give their children what they never had were frightened and hurt to see those children growing further away from them. The hope that had brought them to the New World was for their children even more than for themselves, and if the children did not care, what was left?

. . . when an immigrant's son was lucky enough to graduate from university, he entered a respectable profession like medicine or law or teaching. I opted for art studies and that was unforgivable. Eighteen years would pass before my father made his peace with me. . . W.K.

As the children became adults, most would learn to understand and appreciate their parents again. The parents, in turn, would learn to respect the right of their children to make certain decisions concerning their lives. But the learning on both sides could be painful.

Sharing the Work Load: Even a blacksmith was not above accepting help from his wife.

Men's work, women's work

Although custom decided what was men's work and what was women's work, when it came to helping a husband there was often no such division.

In farm families, the father and his sons did the "heavy" work: the plowing, planting and harvesting, and the mother might do the milking and caring for the chickens until the younger children were old enough to help. She usually had a small vegetable garden near the house from which she provisioned the family table and preserved food for the coming winter. Whatever else she did, a farm wife, like her sister in the city, was expected to do all the housework, prepare the meals and care for the children, helped by her older daughters. She made most of their clothing, mending and cutting down the garments of one child for the next youngest. Since large families were common among farmers, this often meant sewing late into the night.

But in practice, the division between men's work and women's work was far from sharp. Each did what had to be done. A farm mother might also be the extra farmhand, especially during harvest time, the carpenter and woodchopper.

Men sometimes had to do "women's work" too, particularly if the mother were ill, or had to be absent from the house.

. . . a mysterious stomach ailment . . . afflicted my father for an entire summer. He had to look after me as best he could while Mother worked in the fields. At the time, she was probably pregnant with John. . . W.K.

Perhaps the most unusual work for a woman was helping her husband in a blacksmith shop. In 19th-century North America, the horse was the main means of travel and the blacksmith was everywhere. The "smithy" was pictured in poems and paintings as a powerful, muscular man, doing work no "weak woman" could attempt. But in real life — particularly in rural areas — women might swing heavy hammers down on anvils just as they swung heavy axes on chopping blocks.

This family lived in a farming area with poor and rocky soil. Besides shoeing horses, the blacksmith repaired broken wheels, disks and plows. Income was small from this service, so the smith also raised horses, kept milk cows and chickens, and had a garden. His wife and children helped with all of the farm chores, and when there was extra work in the shop, his wife helped there too.

The Taste and Smell of Home: Food linked the kitchen of the New World with that of the Old.

Holding the family together

The immigrant was always in "two places" — the Old Country he longed for and the New World where he lived. It was the immigrant woman, the Mother, who held the two places together, just as she held her family together. Her kitchen where she prepared foods such as her mother had done in Europe — a time-consuming task — was the center of family life and the cosiest room in the house. Here everyone sat, talked and ate while children played or studied.

For Jewish immigrants there was no looking back. Because of the sufferings they had known in Europe — the prejudices, the persecutions, the pogroms, the laws that prevented them from owning land or in some cases even businesses, that kept their children from attending certain schools and universities and banned them from certain professions — they were dedicated to making sure the promised freedoms of the New World were realized. The Friday night dinner and larger family gatherings for weddings and bar-mitzvahs along with annual religious festivals were times of mutual comfort and encouragement.

Preparing for the Sabbath in a Jewish home: Poor families saved all week to lay a feast on Friday evening.

After Church during Indian Summer: A family shares its meal, enjoying the last warm days before winter.

The comfort of religion

. . . There is Someone with me and always has been. And He has asked me to get up because there is work to be done. . . W.K.

Freedom of religion — the right to worship God as one's conscience directed — was the reason many immigrants came to North America. Many of the first settlers in the United States came because of religious persecution at home. Later came the Irish Catholics and Jews. Religious groups, outlawed or persecuted in eastern Europe, Germany and Scandinavia, set up communities. A few of these, notably Mennonite farms in the United States and Canada, continue to this day.

Even when the search for religious freedom was not the main reason for coming, the immigrant was usually a "religious" person. He believed he must pass on to his children the beliefs, the rules and comforts he had grown up with.

The priest or minister was the kindly "father." He baptized and blessed babies, performed weddings and said the prayers at funerals, marking off the stages of life and death. He comforted the sick and bereaved and shared their happiness and good fortune. His visit to the home of a parishioner honored the house, and if he stayed to partake of a family meal, he made it a feast. Many groups — particularly the Irish, Italian and Polish — brought priests from the homeland to man their pulpits, thereby continuing both their religious and national heritages.

Religion could also keep a culture alive when it was threatened with extinction. After the defeat of the French in Quebec in 1759, the Catholic Church there for the next two hundred years became the guardian of traditional values, protecting the French language, educating the children and keeping a distinct identity surrounded by a continent of English-speaking people.

The church was often the first communal building to be built. The Sunday service to which the family wore their best clothes broke the monotony of the six-day work week. At church socials, bazaars and concerts, everyone met to talk, share news and laugh. Christmas, Easter and Thanksgiving, a holiday new to Europeans, were times of joyous celebration.

Because they were so often lonely, afraid and tired, the sense that God was with them gave them courage to endure and to hope.

The Old Country Remembered: Parents recreate the Christmas of their childhood for their own children.

Times to celebrate and be happy

For young and old, Christmas was the highlight of the year. The season itself, with its music and decorations, church services and special foods, lasted for several weeks and brightened the year.

Letters, greetings and even small gifts might go back and forth across the Atlantic as each group tried to imitate the Christmas it had known in the Old Country. In school the children sang carols and often prepared a special choral service to which parents came.

Some might eat the great feast at midnight on Christmas Eve, others on Christmas Day, and still others on "Little Christmas" in January. Gift giving might be at any of those times, or even on New Year's Day. The gifts might be very little — a handful of candies in each child's stocking — but along with the decorations, maybe a tree and candles, and the foods that were only served that day of the year, it was looked forward to by everyone in the family. Children always considered it their special day.

The Polish feast held Christmas Eve is an example of how Old Country customs were kept. The ceremony could not begin until the first star appeared in the sky. Wafers known as "the bread of love" were blessed in the church and then put in the center of the table.
The wife starts the ceremony by offering it to her husband. They break it, eat, embrace and kiss, then the others around the table do the same. Toasts are drunk and twelve main dishes, representing the twelve apostles, are served. Two empty chairs are put at the table, to welcome unexpected guests.

The other happiest time was a wedding. If Christmas was for the intimate family, weddings were for the larger family, including friends who might come long distances for the festivities, dancing and singing. Again the customs, food and music brought a little of the Old World to the New. Although today, most of the children and grandchildren of immigrants have given up attempting to make old country foods in their homes — finding them too time-consuming, they will usually arrange to have them served at weddings, for reasons of sentiment, family continuity and old-fashioned warmth.

A Farm Wedding: The preparations could take months and the festivities could go on for several days.

Relatives traveled great distances to attend as it was a rare chance for a family reunion.

A Business of One's Own. Freedom could mean the right not to have to work for other people.

The dream of independence

One of the freedoms many immigrants sought in North America was the freedom to be one's own boss, to run one's own business.

In many of the European countries they had left, working class people spent their lives working for others with little hope of escape. To be free of that seemed to many to be free indeed.

Because few immigrants had any wealth to bring with them, they had to start in a small way. Usually they worked for others for several years, sometimes taking on night jobs as well as day work, and saved every penny. If the wife worked, her income too was saved toward the "down payment."

Sometimes a husband and wife built a family business together, a small shop with living quarters in the rear or upstairs, and each child, as he grew older, joined the other workers in the family. Because the couple did most of the work between them, these shops came to be known as "mom and pop stores." If the husband died, the widow usually continued to run the enterprise herself with the help of her children.

The business might be small: a grocery store, a soda fountain, a bakery, a machine or tool shop, or even a pushcart. But it was their own. They worked hard, often doing the work of two or three people, and kept their businesses open long hours. One or other of the couple might have to continue to do additional work outside to pay off the purchase. Often such stores were in "immigrant districts" where the owner could serve people from his country in their own language. And sometimes he sold the foods and breads, meats and pastries they had loved in their homeland.

Some took their children from school as soon as the law allowed to help them full-time. But most expected the children to help only after school and on week-ends, serving, running errands, stocking shelves. Children also often earned money on their own, working in other people's stores, selling or delivering newspapers. Many children of immigrants would credit their own success in life to the example of hard work set them by their parents. . .

My father had been hard on his children back on the land. But he had set us all a good example with his own industry. . . W.K.

Worth the Long Hours: One could take pride in a store with faithful customers developed over the years.

And the dream did come true for some.

Wealth was possible for a few, for those who could build small businesses into larger ones or small farms into big ones.

Even those immigrants who never earned enough to escape the drudgery of hard work themselves usually had the satisfaction of seeing their children better off.

. . . Father had planned and dreamed for years to make something of his children by means of higher education. . . W.K.

For most immigrants, giving their children a better education than they had was their first goal and they were ready to give up personal comforts to achieve it, encouraging their children to study and taking pride and pleasure in their accomplishments.

Most had the satisfaction of seeing at least a partial fulfillment of the hopes and dreams that had brought them to North America. They had claimed a part of the New World for themselves. Their children would reinforce that claim, and their grandchildren would continue to complete the dream.

They helped shape the North America of today as much as they were shaped by it.

Looking Back. For a fortunate few, success came beyond anything they ever dreamed possible.

Looking Ahead: Others would continue to hope for a better life for their children and grandchildren.

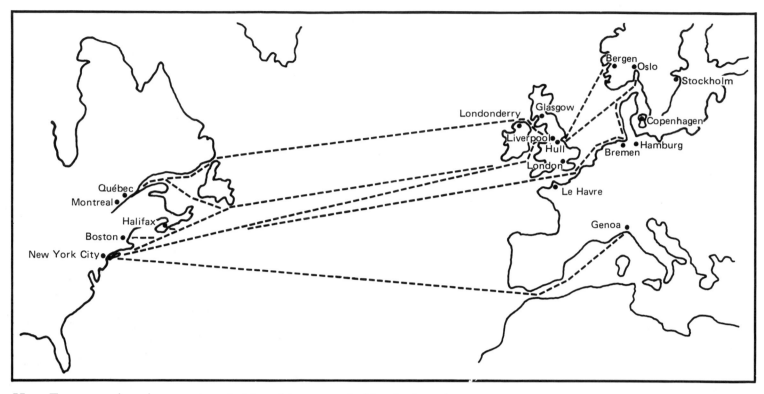

How European immigrants traveled by ship to reach North American ports

U.S. immigration from Europe 1820-1979   Total 36,267,000
Germany 6,985,000; Italy 5,300,000; Great Britain 4,948,000; Ireland 4,691,000; Austria
4,317,000; Soviet Union 3,375,000; Sweden 1,273,000; Norway 857,000; France 753,000;
Greece 661,000; Poland 581,000; Portugal 452,000; Denmark 365,000; Netherlands 361,000;
Switzerland 350,000; Spain 263,000; Belgium 203,000; Czechoslovakia 138,000; Yugoslavia
115,000; Finland 34,000; other European countries 308,000. (Figures taken from U.S.
Immigration and Naturalization Service, Annual Report.)

European origins of the Canadian population based on 1971 census.
British (including Irish) 9,624,115; total other European 11,139,800 made up as follows:
French 6,180,120; German 1,317,200; Italian 730,820; Ukrainian 580,660; Netherlander
425,945; Scandinavian 384,795; Polish 316,430; Jewish 296,945 — countries not given;
Norwegian 179,290; Hungarian 131,890; Greek 124,475; Yugoslavic 104,955; Swedish 101,870;
Czech and Slovak 81,870; Danish 75,725; Russian 64,675; Finnish 59,215; Belgian 51,135;
Austrian 42,120; Icelandic 27,905; Romanian 27,375; Lithuanian 24,535; other European
194,850. Note: Up to 1911, Danish, Icelandic, Norwegian and Swedish immigrants were
counted in the Scandinavian total. (Figures taken from Historical Statistics of Canada,
Second Edition.)

48